IN-LINE SKATING
BASICS

IN-LINE SKATING
SKATING
BASICS

Cam Millar

Photographed by
Bruce Curtis

Sterling Publishing Co., Inc.
New York

Library of Congress Cataloging-in-Publication Data

Millar, Cam.
   In-line skating basics   /   by Cam Millar & Bruce Curtis.
     p.   cm.
     Includes index.
     ISBN 0-8069-3849-8
     1. In-line skating.   I. Curtis, Bruce.   II. Title.
   GV859.73.M545   1995
   792.2′1—dc20   95-30965
                                                CIP

Designed by Judy Morgan

3   5   7   9   10   8   6   4   2

First paperback edition published in 1996 by
Sterling Publishing Company, Inc.
387 Park Avenue South, New York, N.Y. 10016
© 1996 by Cam Millar and Bruce Curtis
Distributed in Canada by Sterling Publishing
c/o Canadian Manda Group, One Atlantic Avenue, Suite 105
Toronto, Ontario, Canada M6K 3E7
Distributed in Great Britain and Europe by Cassell PLC
Wellington House, 125 Strand, London WC2R 0BB, England
Distributed in Australia by Capricorn Link (Australia) Pty Ltd.
P.O. Box 6651, Baulkham Hills, Business Centre, NSW 2153, Australia
Printed in Hong Kong
All rights reserved

Sterling ISBN 0-8069-3849-8 Trade
0-8069-3851-X Paper

CONTENTS

PREFACE

In less than ten years, in-line skating has become an international sport, enjoyed by people of all ages, shapes, and sizes. And in the space of just a few short years, in-line speed skating, in-line hockey, in-line ramp and vertical skating, in-line street skating, in-line figure skating, in-line slalom skating, in-line dancing, and in-line aerobic fitness classes have become phenominally popular. This book is about the common denominator among these activities: in-line skating basics.

The concepts in this book are time-tested; they're based on ice-skating technique as applied to in-line skates. Practice of the exercises contained in this book will provide a sound base for balance, technique, and confidence of movement, which you can build upon as you move on to more advanced forms of in-line skating.

If you work your way through this book, practise the techniques shown, and have a competent instructor check on your progress, you can become a solid in-line skater, able to tackle any terrain with speed, balance, agility, grace, and confidence.

Thanks to photographer Bruce Curtis for his patience and his great sense of humor. Thanks also to Marsha Genensky for helping me to get my ideas down on paper, Liz Marino for her line drawing, Margarett Dykstra for her inspirational teaching, Randy at Blades Second Avenue, New York, N.Y., Jennifer at Fritz's Skate Shop in Miami, and all of the skating students with whom I have worked.

INTRODUCTION

In-line skating has made such a positive, healthful impact on such a large number of people that governmental leaders have actually adjusted city plans to accommodate it and its participants. It's a low-impact sport that makes possible aerobic, anaerobic, cardiovascular, fat- and calorie-burning, strength-training regimens.

In-line skating requires a very small cash outlay and is well worth the money when measured in terms of improvement in physical and mental health. It not only provides a great workout, but it also offers many people the chance to express themselves in new ways. Whether you live in a city or in the country, you'll experience the universal appeal of gliding. As you gain control over your skates, you'll discover your own style.

To become a strong in-line skater takes work and practice; but mastery of the basics and fundamentals of skating will lead to a lifetime of enjoyment. The beginner can follow the sequence of this book and start with the most basic aspects of skating, and move on later to more advanced maneuvers.

It is important to remember that no two people progress at the same rate. Please be kind to yourself! When learning to skate, the maxim should be, "If there's any pain, then there's surely no gain." You'll discover that skating uses very specific muscles that can only be strengthened while you're actually on your skates.

This book contains technical information on the physical mechanics of skating and gives hints that will lead you to feel the movements required to perform each exercise with confidence. The photos are laid out so that you can observe proper technique and form.

One important note: before you begin, please put on your protective equipment. You'll feel much more confident about trying new moves when you know that you've taken precautions in order to

prevent skinned knees and elbows or broken bones. It's inevitable that you'll fall sometime when on your skates. But in-line protective equipment is well designed, and it *does* work!

Finally, the greatest gift you can give yourself is to find a caring, competent, qualified in-line instructor. All Olympic ice-skating champions have coaches. These athletes skate at the highest level every day for hours on end, but they know that remaining under a watchful eye is essential for their continued safety, growth, and success. And what is it that their coaches watch for? *Basics!*

HISTORY

Although modern in-line skates were introduced about one hundred years later than traditional double-axle quad roller skates, they are more direct descendants of ancient ice skates than they are of quad skates. Our early ancestors attached slender animal bones or antlers to their boots to travel across icy territory. Northern Europeans gradually refined this design to the point that the modern ice blade hasn't really changed in shape or form for several hundred years.

The double-axle roller skate was invented by an American, J.L. Plimpton, in 1863; it is unclear who was the real inventor of the modern in-line skate. Ralph Backstrom, one of the fastest skaters of his time who played for the Montréal Canadiens of the National Hockey League in the 1960s, made a

version of an in-line skate in order to train during the off-season.

Around 1980, Scott Olsen came across a pair of in-line skates in a sporting-goods store in Minnesota, and realized that they would be perfect for his off-season hockey training. After building some skates for his own use and for the use of his friends, he began to experiment with various modifications. Realizing that there was great interest not only among his local hockey-playing friends but among off-season cross-country skiers and a now-interested general public as well, he built a small business, which eventually grew into Rollerblade, Inc.

It wasn't long before several other companies saw the huge growth potential of the sport of in-line skating. In 1995, in-line skating became a billion-dollar business.

With the increased popularity of in-line skating came special-interest organizations. The International In-Line Skating Association (IISA), created in 1991, keeps in touch with large manufacturers in order to maintain awareness of consumer needs and to promote safety. The IISA also has a committee that deals with municipal concerns and the public image of in-line skating and in-line skaters, and has established the Instructor Certification Program, the only recognized training program for in-line skating instructors.

In-line skate clubs have sprung up in cities around the world. These clubs disseminate information on special events of interest to their members, sponsor various local and national series speed-skating races, and help to keep club members in touch with some of the latest developments in the in-line world.

Freestyle, ramp, vertical, and street skaters have become well organized in America; 1994 was the first year of competitions in these areas under the banner of the National In-Line Skate Series (NISS). Most professional events are now sanctioned under the ASA (Aggressive Skating Association).

In-line speed skating now attracts top Olympic ice skaters who race and use in-line skates for off-ice training. In 1996, in-line racing will be an exhibition sport at the Summer Olympics in Atlanta.

Special mention must be made of the phenomenal growth of in-line hockey in America. In 1993, certain areas of the country saw more children registering for roller hockey than for little-league baseball, and adult leagues have as many participants as do the youth leagues. USA Hockey, the national governing body for ice hockey in the United States, is now dedicated to proper training of coaches and officials for in-line hockey. Professional hockey is represented by the RHI; both USA Hockey and the NIHA (National In-Line Hockey Association) manage amateur leagues throughout North America.

In-line skaters develop and define in-line skating, and continue to write the history of the sport.

BEFORE
YOU START

WHO CAN SKATE?

If you were to pay a visit to an area popular for in-line skating, you would see an amazing variety of people in various stages of progress: people from an extremely wide age range, men, women, and children, with all the world's different ethnicities represented. In-line skating seems to have almost universal appeal.

Those gifted with athletic talent and who are accustomed to regular participation in fitness or sports activities may find that they become proficient on in-line skates within a short period of time.

For those who haven't been as active: Watch a class of beginners on their in-line skates for the first time. People of all ages, shapes, and sizes are taking their first awkward steps; the spectacle draws laughter from the participants. Come back in ten minutes and watch the class again and you'll see a group of people skating!

Unless you've had a back or spinal surgery, or unless you have a severe inner-ear problem or other physical handicap that makes retaining your sense of balance difficult, you should have no problem becoming a successful in-line skater!

WHAT DO YOU NEED?

Skates When you visit an in-line skate specialty store, or any sporting-goods store that sells skates and related equipment, the choices available may at first seem overwhelming. Unless you go with a friend who knows about in-line skates, find a salesperson to help explain the various models.

In-line skates can be divided into several categories:
- recreational, fitness, and hockey skates (adult and children)
- speed skates
- street and stunt skates
- specialty cross-training skates

For the beginning in-line skater, recreational and fitness skates are most appropriate, although a good hockey skate can also be used for general skating. As your skating improves, you'll find that a good recreational, fitness, or hockey skate will also enable you to get the feel for and participate in most other forms of in-line skating.

As is true when purchasing other sporting-goods equipment, you get what you pay for. The better manufacturers use good materials and make it easy for you to get replacement parts for your skates. Ask the salesperson if the particular model you're thinking of buying is backed up by

Recreational skates

the store and by the manufacturer. Boots and frames of high-quality in-line skates can last for years. Despite the technology available, some manufacturers use inferior materials, so don't be lured by an advertisement for an inexpensive skate. Beginners and professionals all need proper ankle and arch support. A few hours in the wrong boots can make you miserable!

You won't be a beginner for very long! For the extra money spent on good-quality skates, you'll be buying:

- superior wheels and bearings
- strong and lightweight frames
- the proper combination of ankle support and flexibility
- strong, durable inner and outer boot material
- buckles that will stay fastened
- the option to modify your skates in order to participate in other in-line disciplines

Three- and four-wheel skates

Skates come with 4 wheels (men's and medium and large women's sizes; some children's) or with 3 (some small women's or children's sizes). The number of wheels on your skates won't affect your skating ability or your enjoyment of in-line skating.

FIT

When trying on skates, be sure to wear either cotton or wool socks of thin or medium thickness. After you've put each skate on, lightly bang your heel on the floor in order to drive your heel to the back of the boot. Tie your laces or fasten your buckles until they're moderately tight. Be sure that the laces or buckles are done up properly. Now stand up and bend your knees in order to drive your heels even farther back into the boots. If, when you bend your knees, your heels feel as if they are coming up in the boots, try a smaller size.

Once you've found boots that hold your heels snugly in place, make sure that your toes are free to wiggle around. Your toes may brush very lightly against the end of the boots, but they shouldn't be pinched together or jammed against the end of the boots. Do some deep knee bends to get an idea of how your feet will feel when you're in skating position.

Finally, before making your purchase, try on several pairs of skates to be sure of getting the best fit.

The better in-line manufacturers have designed women's versions of their more popular men's skate models. Women's skates generally have a lower rear cuff; some are specially designed for narrow feet.

The better manufacturers have also created excellent children's skates. Children *need* proper ankle support, so don't buy skates that are two sizes too big with the idea that your child will grow into his or her skates. Wearing skates that are too large is very dangerous. Excellent children's skates are modestly priced, and with the huge public interest in skating, you may be able to find excellent used skates that another child has recently outgrown.

RENTAL EQUIPMENT

If you plan to rent skates in order to see if you like in-line skating, be sure to check the following:
- skates have all of their buckles intact
- boots have strong, proper support
- boots aren't cracked
- wheels aren't loose
- brakes aren't worn down
- laces aren't broken or too short

If you follow the advice for getting a proper fit, you should have an enjoyable time. If you like the skates that you're wearing, make note of the model name and skate size.

Protective Gear

It's likely that most or all of your in-line skating activity will take place on a concrete, asphalt, brick, wood, or rubber surface. Bare skin will not slide on these surfaces! The result: "road rash" (broken skin) or broken bones.

Preventing road rash is very simple. In-line protective gear has plastic fittings that enable you to slide a little bit upon hitting the ground and foam or rubber backing that helps to absorb the impact of a fall.

Wrist guards, elbow pads, knee pads, and helmet: this protective gear is designed extremely well. If you wear protective equipment, you'll be

able to try new maneuvers and techniques with full concentration on your skating, and without risking getting hurt in the occasional but inevitable fall.

WRIST GUARDS

There are several variations in wrist-guard design. The common element is the plastic "skid pad" worn on the palm of the hand. The lightest wrist guards incorporate the skid pad in a driving-glove design. Other guards have an additional piece of plastic covering the top of the hand, wrist, and part of the forearm which prevents the wrist from bending too far backwards. Yet other wrist guards give even more protection to other parts of the hand. All of these wrist guards will protect the palms of your hands, allow for flexion of the wrists, and make it possible for your arms to slide upon impact with the ground.

Skater with protective gear

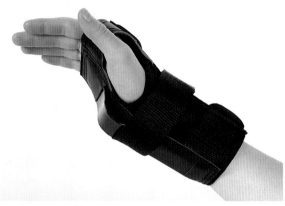

Standard wrist guard

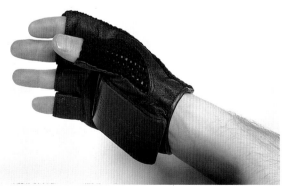

Skid pad or driving-glove wrist guard

ELBOW PADS

Elbow-pad design is very similar among manufacturers. Make sure that your elbow pads cover the sides of your elbows and fasten securely.

KNEE PADS

Knee-pad design is very similar among manufacturers. Make sure that your knee pads offer some wrap-around protection to the side of the knees and that they fasten securely.

Standard elbow guard

Various styles of helmet

CLOTHING

An important consideration when you go skating is your choice of clothing. You can dress in your own style, but make sure that your clothes allow a good range of motion in your legs, arms, and upper body. Your clothing should also allow for air exchange for cooling your body. Cotton clothes, specialty sporting clothes, and bicycle-style shorts work equally well. If you must wear baggy pants, don't overdo it. They will actually hinder your skating if they are too long and heavy.

Don't wear your bikini. Please make sure that your hips are covered, as they are especially susceptible to "road rash." You may also want to think about making sure that your shoulders, upper back and upper arms are covered in case of a slide.

Standard knee pads

HELMETS

The main reason for wearing a helmet is obvious. Another important advantage of wearing a helmet is that it makes you much more visible when you're skating in traffic or congested areas. You can make yourself even more visible by putting bright-colored reflective safety markings on your helmet.

Helmet design has come a long way both in terms of fashion and in terms of effectiveness. Although in-line companies make their own helmets, you can also use bicycle or skiing helmets. Make sure that your helmet meets required government safety regulations.

WHERE CAN YOU SKATE?

One of the great things about in-line skating is that as you become a strong skater you'll always be able to seek out new skating territory. Some people have even skated across the United States!

In order to find out about the best skating spots in your area, inquire at an in-line skate shop. Find out the name of your local in-line club, or stop skaters on the street and ask them where they like to skate. They may also know about the best areas for learning and practising.

Every city, suburban, or rural area will offer a variety of appropriate places for you to skate. Consider the following possibilities:

- in-line skate parks or arenas
- ice-skating arenas (off-season)
- gymnasiums, indoor and outdoor running tracks
- bicycle paths, civic parks (where allowed)
- beachfront boardwalks
- golf-course cart paths (if allowed)
- shopping-center parking lots, industrial parks (after hours)
- rural roadways
- streets (for strong, experienced skaters)

Use your common sense! When learning, stay in areas that give you the freedom to experiment and practise while retaining full control of your abilities.

WHEN CAN YOU SKATE?

Weather & Road Conditions

You can skate whenever the roads are dry, but please take the following precautions:

Drink plenty of fluid before, during, and after your workout, especially in hot weather. Specialty sports drinks are well suited to in-line skaters; the best formulas replenish and provide the proper nutrients and fluids for proper muscle usage, efficiency, and recovery during strenuous exercise.

signs of rain, head for the nearest bench and take your skates off.

Even when the roads are dry, watch for small twigs, loose dirt and sand, pebbles, loose leaves, and oil slicks from cars and trucks. In colder weather, stay alert for patches of "black ice," which may either be hidden in the shadows or invisible because of poor light reflection. In general, avoid areas with small, loose debris.

In hot, humid weather, dress so that your body can cool off properly. Wear good sunglasses with proper UV protection.

There is no reason why you can't skate year-round as long as the roads are dry. In winter, wear warm clothing, dress in layers, and start slowly to give your muscles a chance to warm up.

Skating in wet conditions is bad for the life of your skates. But more important, skating in wet weather is hazardous, even for the most experienced skater. In-line skates skid and slip on wet surfaces. Even in the lightest rainfall, sand, dirt, and oil slicks add to the danger. So, at the first

Physical Condition & Mental Alertness

You must be healthy and mentally alert when you skate, whether you're working out or trying to get somewhere.

Don't skate if you've been injured: You don't want to worsen your injury. Don't skate when physically exhausted; this can lead to serious accidents.

When skating, you must be able to make instant decisions on stopping, turning, and in choosing the safest routes *while* you are in motion. There is an incredible amount of information to process when you're on your skates, and your body is working much harder than you realize. Please evaluate your physical condition and mental awareness before you take to the streets.

GETTING
STARTED

BASIC RULES

Before you begin each skating session:
Check your skates. Make sure they don't have loose axles, wobbly or stuck wheels, or broken buckles.

Make sure your skates are properly laced or buckled.

Make sure your wrist guards, knee pads, elbow pads, and helmet are securely fastened.

Things to remember when you're skating:
If at any time you feel off-balance or out of control on your skates, bring your hands to your knees. By doing this, you make sure that your knees are lightly bent and that your upper body is in a slightly forward position. This will prevent you from falling backwards.

Eyes and head up, knees bent, relaxed!

Your knees should be bent at all times. Some exercises and maneuvers only require you to keep your knees slightly bent; others require you to lower yourself into a sitting position.

To check that your knees are bent enough: make sure that you feel the front of your ankle leaning against the tongue of your skate.

Feel that your center of gravity is in your hips.

Try to keep your weight on the balls of your feet.

Keep your eyes and head up at all times. You'll find that looking in the direction in which you intend to skate will help you to travel safely and easily.

No matter how difficult you find a particular exercise, try not to get tense. The more relaxed and focused you are, the more easily you'll master the maneuver.

Bring your hands to your knees when off-balance

The more you practise each of the exercises in this book, the better. You may find it helpful to spend time practising them without your skates as well as with them.

FIRST MOVES

If you're skating outdoors, find a grassy area near a large, smooth, flat paved area. Make sure the paved area is free of loose debris, sand, and gravel. If you're skating indoors, in an arena or skating complex, start on a nearby carpeted or rubberized area. You must first get a "feel" for your in-line skates on a surface that will prevent you from rolling freely. Start with some simple balancing exercises.

The "dry-land" start (on grass, carpeted area)
Before you begin: Check skates, make sure they don't have loose axles, wobbly or stuck wheels, or broken buckles.

Make sure skates are properly laced or buckled.

Make sure wrist guards, knee pads, elbow pads, and helmet are securely fastened.

If you're sitting on a bench, stand up slowly. Rest with your hands on your knees, making sure that your knees are bent. If you're starting from the ground, move onto your knees, then stand up one foot at a time. Stand and rest with hands on knees. Do a couple of easy knee bends.

Next, stand with your feet comfortably shoulder-width apart, knees bent. Take an easy step forward. Step back to the starting position, keeping your knees slightly bent. Repeat this action several times with each leg.

Beginner's stance: hands on knees

Lunging on the grass

The "V" walk (duck-walk) on grass or on a carpeted

area Remaining on the grass or carpeted area, stand with your feet comfortably apart and knees bent. Now, maneuver both feet into a turned-out, "V" stance.

Begin to walk with your feet in this position, keeping your knees slightly bent. Keep your head and eyes up, and bring your arms out in front of you for balance.

Spend some time on the grass or carpet, and experiment with your mobility. Try lunges of various sizes, keeping your knees bent, and your head and eyes up.

Don't rush from grass to concrete! After spending time on the nonslippery surfaces, you'll see how easy it is to get up and move on the skating surface.

Try these small lunges again, this time concentrating on the muscles supporting you on your front leg, just above your knee. Now, as you lunge forward, bring your upper body (chest) over your knee. Repeat the action, focusing on your pelvic region. Feel the strength and balance that you gain as you focus on these muscles.

"V" walk on grass

1

2

3

4

Onto the skating surface

Now you should have a pretty good feel for standing and walking in your skates.

If you're starting from the grass, approach the skating surface one skate at a time, remaining parallel to the surface. Step onto the surface with bent knees, one foot at a time.

If you're in a skating arena surrounded by a wall or boards, hang onto the boards or railing and step onto the surface.

How to fall

Before you begin to skate, you must learn how to fall, and you must learn how to get up and back into skating position.

With your hands on your knees, bend your knees until you're close enough to the ground that you can lower yourself onto your knee pads. You won't hurt yourself! Knee pads are very well designed.

Now that you're on your knees, bring your palms in front of you and make contact with the plastic slider on the wrist guard. In an actual fall, you

A good fall! A forward fall!

could now safely slide right onto your elbow pads as well. This falling exercise shows that your protective gear works.

Getting up
Now stand up, one foot at a time. Rest one or both hands on your standing knee as you rise. Placing your hands on your knees will ensure that your knees are slightly bent and will allow you to regain your balance.

"V" walk on skating surface

Getting up after a fall

"V" walk on the skating surface
Assume the position of hands-on-knees, feet shoulder-width apart. Raise your arms up to about waist level. Keeping your eyes up, begin a series of very small weight shifts from one leg to the other. Feel this action as originating in your pelvic region.

While continuing this small weight shift, begin to turn your toes out into the "V" position. Now you're skating!

Hands-to-knees & glide

Take three or four steps, bring your legs back to a comfortable, shoulder-width position, and put your hands on your knees. Go for a glide!

While gliding, raise your arms again and turn your toes back out into the "V" position in preparation for a few more steps. After another three or four steps, bring your hands back to your knees and go for another glide.

Beginner's stop Now that you're up and rolling, you should know how to slow down to stop.

Bring your legs into a comfortable gliding position. Next, bring them to more than shoulder-width apart, bending your knees at the same time. Lower yourself and point your toes inward. Remain in this lowered (almost sitting) position until you come to a stop.

BUILDING A STRONG FOUNDATION

The inside edge: ballet exercise

Stand facing a wall or the boards of an arena. Turn your toes out into the "V" position. Now, step back about a foot or so with your toes in this turned-out position. Place your hands on the wall or boards, and lean against it. Imagine that you're trying to push the wall forward. If your toes are turned out in a "V," you'll notice that you're pushing into the ground with the *inside edges* of the wheels.

Do a few pliés, or knee bends. Continue to feel the inside edges pushing against the ground. Step back enough so that you can really lean into the wall.

The outside edge

When your knees come together, you roll onto your inside edges. As you move your knees apart, you roll onto your *outside edges*.

The terms *inside* and *outside edges* will be used throughout the book and are important for your understanding of more advanced skating mechanics and maneuvers.

Inside edges

Outside edges

Ballet exercise

Right-push, glide; left-push, glide

Start with your knees bent and your feet close together in the "V" position. Bring your arms up in front of you, bend your knees more, and give a strong push with one leg. Feel the inside edge push into the ground. Bring your feet back into parallel position and glide, with your hands on your knees.

As you glide, prepare to give a push with your other leg. Turn that leg out in the "V" position, bend your knees more, and give a good, strong push. Bring your feet back into parallel position and glide, bringing your hands back to your knees.

Glide

Right-push . . .

TIPS

→ Make sure that you bend your knees enough to generate enough power for your pushes. To be sure your knees are adequately bent, feel that the front of your ankle presses against the tongue of each skate.

→ If you're having trouble, go back to the ballet exercise to get the feeling of pushing with the inside edges.

Deep knee bends

After doing the push-glide exercise, bring your feet as close together as possible and bend your knees deeply.

As you lower and raise yourself during the knee bend, focus on remaining balanced, centered, and on top of your skates. Only bend down as far as is comfortable. Don't force yourself to lean too far forward.

As your skating muscles become stronger, you'll be able to keep your legs close together during deep knee bends.

Trusting each leg

The art of skating is essentially that of balancing and gliding on one leg at a time. It's important to be able to stand, push, and glide equally well on each leg.

Start to practise this now. Start with your feet shoulder-width apart, with your knees slightly bent.

Begin to shift your weight from one leg to the other. As you continue this action, bend your knees more and begin to feel how you can shift a large percentage of your weight onto each leg.

Concentrate on your pelvic area. As you shift to the right, the majority of your weight shifts onto your right hip. As you shift to the left, the majority of your weight will shift to your left hip.

Small glides on one leg

Now you can combine pushing with the inside edge and lunging. With your knees bent, turn your feet into the "V" stance and push with your right leg. As you push, take a small lunge forward, allowing your weight to shift onto your left hip and your left leg.

and give a push with your left skate. As soon as your skate leaves the ground, center your balance over your right leg. As always, feel the center of gravity and balance through the hip of your supporting leg.

Return your left skate to the ground. Give a push with your right skate, and shift your weight over your left leg. Stay relaxed and focused.

Glide with leg raise

Do some pushes and glides. As you glide, make sure that your knees are bent, your head and eyes are up, and you are travelling in a straight line.

Shift your weight slightly onto your right leg,

Glides plus strokes become strides

strides If you watch an experienced skater moving in a straight line, it seems as if he or she never has both skates on the ground at the same time. This is almost true, but the only difference between the way an accomplished skater moves and what you have been practising is that the experienced skater has minimized the amount of time that both skates remain in contact with the skating surface.

Begin the right-push, glide, left-push, glide exercise. But this time, after you have pushed with your right skate, bring it back into gliding position, almost simultaneously moving your left skate into its "V" position. Concentrate on spending less time preparing for your next push. Now you're beginning to stride.

STOPPING

BRAKING—STEP-BY-STEP

Almost all models of in-line skates have a rubber heel brake, most often mounted on the right skate. The easiest and safest way to slow yourself down or to stop on in-line skates is to use this brake. To learn how to come to a safe stop using your heel brake, you must master the following four steps.

Two-foot parallel glide
While gliding, bring your feet to a parallel position, about 4–6″ apart. Make sure that your knees are bent, your eyes and head are up, arms are up in front of you, and that you're travelling in a straight line.

Brake foot in front
From the two-foot parallel glide, move your braking foot forward so that the heel of your braking foot is at least opposite the toe of your other skate.

All of your wheels should be in contact with the ground. Your knees are still bent, eyes are up, arms are in front of you, and you're travelling in a straight line with your feet about 4–6″ apart.

Heel brake makes contact
With your braking foot in front of you, lift the toe slowly so that the heel brake makes contact with the ground.

Step One: two-foot parallel glide

Step Two: brake foot in front!

Step Three: heel brake makes contact with ground

Step Four: "sit" into brake and push heel into ground

Once you feel your heel brake make contact with the ground, hold this position as you glide. This is what it feels like to use the heel brake to make contact with the skating surface without disrupting your balance.

As before, your knees are bent, your eyes are up, arms are in front of you, and your feet are still 4–6 inches apart.

Sitting into the brake
Begin to lower yourself (sit down), at the same time putting more pressure onto your heel brake as you push it into the ground.

How to practise steps 2–4
Scissoring is good practice for step 2. From a stationary position with knees bent, slide your right foot in front of your left; as you bring it back, slide your left foot in front of your right. Repeat the exercise, alternating feet.

Rolling onto the grass is good practice for steps 3–4. Find an area in which you can safely glide from the skating surface onto a grassy area or carpeted or rubber surface which is free from debris.

Approach the grass or carpet with your braking foot well in front of you and roll onto it, seeing how far you can glide in this position. If you are standing too straight, the impact of rolling onto the grass will throw you off balance. So make sure that your knees are well bent and that you are well supported on your rear leg.

PUTTING IT ALL TOGETHER

Practise the four steps from a stationary position.
1. Bring your feet together (4–6″ apart).
2. Slide braking foot in front. This skate should be at least opposite the toe of your other skate.
3. Lift up the toe of your braking foot, allowing your brake to make contact with the ground.
4. Lower yourself into a sitting position.
   Here's the complete braking procedure:
   Now try braking from a glide.

Tips

▷ Some beginning skaters have better balance with their right foot in front; others with their left in front. If you're having trouble learning to brake with your right foot, switch your heel brake to the left skate, and try learning to brake with your left.

▷ Don't rotate your upper body, as this will cause your skates to turn, throwing you off balance!

▷ Finish the stop! Come to a complete stop every time you attempt to brake. This is the only way to build your strength and your confidence in your braking ability. Sit down and stay down!

If you're a very strong skater and do your skating in crowded urban conditions, you should be concerned with fast, safe transportation on your in-line skates. You may want to purchase an extra brake assembly and learn to stop on either foot. This will help you to stop safely under any conditions.

THE SWIZZLE

Called *swizzling*, *sculling*, or *ins-and-outs*, this exercise should be mastered before you move onto any other in-line skating maneuvers. The swizzle is an extremely important foundation exercise: it builds strength, improves balance, and forces you to use your inside edges.

Stand with your knees bent, your toes in the "V" position, and your arms up in front of you. Bend your knees even more, push into the ground with the inside edges of both skates, and lean slightly forward with your upper body. This pushing action with both inside edges will move your legs into a shoulder-width (or wider) position. Point your toes inward to bring your feet together again.

To continue, bring your feet fairly close together, bend your knees again as you point your toes outward, and push with both inside edges into the ground.

Once you can swizzle continuously and smoothly, try alternating between swizzling and striding. You'll notice an improvement in your ease of striding and overall balance as you change from the swizzle into alternate-leg stroking.

1 2

Swizzle

3

4

5

TIPS

- If you're having trouble, go back to the ballet exercise (p. 34) to remind yourself of the feeling of pushing with your inside edges.
- Be sure to bend your knees sufficiently. You should be almost in a sitting position.

THE ROCKING HORSE

This exercise consists of alternating one forward swizzle and one backward swizzle.

Do a forward swizzle. Glide to the position where your toes are pointing inward. Now, push into your inside edges while putting more pressure on the balls of your feet. As you push your inside edges away from you, you'll begin to move backwards. Bend your knees more, and push into the ground with the balls of your feet. Roll backwards off of your toes on the inside edges of your skates. Practice this exercise as often as you can.

Backward swizzle

GETTING
AROUND

Turning is one of the greatest pleasures of in-line skating! Regardless of whether you're turning at low or high speed, basic turning principles will help you conquer any terrain.

THE PARALLEL TURN

STEP-BY-STEP

Parallel turn

Corresponding edges

Stand with your feet about 4–6″ apart. Lean your knees, ankles, and skates to your right. Your left skate is on its inside edge, and the right skate is on its outside edge.

Lean your knees, ankles, and skates to the left.

Now your right skate is in its inside edge and your left skate is on its outside edge.

When you're on the inside edge of one skate and the outside edge of the other skate, you're on *corresponding edges*.

Upper-body rotation

Stand with your feet about 4–6″ apart. Relax your rib cage and upper body. Bring your arms up at your sides.

Leading with your eyes, turn your head and look over your right shoulder. Look as far as possible while remaining comfortable, balanced, and relaxed. Now, leading with your eyes, turn your head and look back over your left shoulder as far as possible. As you repeat this action a number of times, you'll find that you'll be able to look farther and farther over each shoulder. As you turn your head from one side to the other, your upper body will begin to follow.

Now, as you rotate to your left, swing your right arm in front of you to the left as well. Allow your left arm and shoulder to swing back as you do this. As you rotate to the right, swing your left arm in front of you and to the right, and allow your right arm and shoulder to swing back. Remember to initiate the rotation with your eyes and head, as you look in the direction of your intended rotation.

As you repeat the action, you'll feel that as your upper body turns, your hips will follow. Your knees are now starting to turn as well. Your skates will shift onto their corresponding edges.

The leading leg into the parallel turn

From a glide, bring your feet to a parallel position about 4–6″ apart. Scissor your right foot forward. Look to the right, allowing your upper body to rotate to the right as well. Bring your left arm across to the right, allow your right shoulder to swing back and your hips and knees to turn to the right. Move onto your corresponding edges, and you're executing a perfect parallel turn to the right. Now try the same thing to the left.

THE SCOOTER

This exercise reinforces proper turning technique, and is a real strength builder. You should spend a good deal of time perfecting it before trying crossovers.

Stand with your body rotated to the left. Imagine a circle drawn on the ground. Your left skate is going to stay on the circle as your right leg does the pushing as you move counterclockwise around the circle.

Start with your left skate on the circle and your right skate in a turned-out position. As you begin to push with the inside edge of your right skate, shift your weight onto your left leg. Your left knee should be bent so that your knee is positioned over your toes, and your eyes, head, and upper body should be rotated to the left (in the direction of travel). After you push with your right skate, bring it back up alongside your left skate, glide for a moment, and give another inside-edge push from your right skate.

Continue to push yourself around the circle with your right leg, centering your weight over your left.

Now try scootering clockwise around a circle, centering your weight over your right leg, and pushing with your left.

Scootering to the left

▐▶ To stay in your imaginary circle as you scooter, focus on a point across the circle.

▐▶ To help with rotation in a scooter to the left, bring your right arm forward and your left arm back. Imagine that you're embracing the imaginary circle. When scootering to the right, bring your left arm forward and your right arm back.

▐▶ Rest often, and change your direction of travel often. Scootering is a real muscle builder, and will quickly tire you out if you overdo it.

Trusting your inside leg When
you turn to the left, your left leg is called the *inside*
leg. When you turn to the right, your right leg is
your *inside* leg. Your inside leg must be able to hold
your body weight during turns, especially during
more advanced maneuvers such as front and back
crossovers as well.

To build strength, balance, and trust in your
inside leg, practise a scooter to the left, trying to
see how long you can glide on your inside leg. Stay
balanced over your left leg, and take your weight in
your left hip. Continue with good strong right
inside-edge pushes. See how far you can travel
around the circle on your inside leg.

Change directions and see how far you can
travel around the circle on your right inside leg.

Learn to trust your inside leg (left inside leg)

EVEN STRONGER SKATING

Smooth crossover technique is important for mobility. Crossovers allow you to make turns without losing momentum; they are essential for many advanced skating forms.

Stationary crossovers
Stand with your feet comfortably shoulder-width apart. Rotate your upper body to the left. Make sure that your knees are bent and that your toes are relaxed.

Shift your weight to your left leg. Pick up your right foot and cross it over your left. As you step with your right foot, make sure that your knees are still bent. Then, bring your left foot back alongside your right, allowing your center of balance to shift back to center. Shift your weight to your left side again and repeat the crossover of your right foot. Now practise picking up your left foot and crossing it over your right.

Stationary right-over-left crossover

TIPS

⟱➡ Keep your crossover foot low to the ground.

⟱➡ Point the toe of your crossover foot in the direction in which it is moving.

Crossovers in motion

Right-over-left: Begin to scooter counterclockwise around a circle. Your knees should be bent and your eyes, head, and upper body should be rotated to the left. Your weight should be on your inside leg.

Lift your right foot just high enough to pass easily over your left skate, pointing your toe into the direction of the turn. As you step down, allow the ball of your foot to make the first contact with the ground. Bring your left leg back alongside the right and go for a short glide. Repeat the action.

Left-over right: begin with a clockwise scooter, and when you feel comfortable, lift your left skate and cross it over your right.

Right-over-left crossovers

Left-over-right crossovers

Figure eights

This maneuver consists of one circle of right-over-left crossovers followed by one circle of left-over-right crossovers. The two circles follow the shape of the number 8.

Visualize on the ground a figure eight consisting of two medium-sized circles. Begin by scootering counterclockwise around the first circle. Your eyes, head, and upper body should be rotated to the left, in the direction of travel. Your weight should be on your inside leg. Use your arms to hug the circle, your right arm forward and your left arm back.

After you complete one circle, rotate your eyes, head, and upper body to the right, the new direction of travel. Shift your weight to your right leg, the new inside leg, and scooter clockwise around the second circle, hugging it with your arms as you do so.

Once you're comfortable scootering around the figure eight, try it with crossovers. Travel the first circle counterclockwise with right-over-left crossovers; travel the second clockwise with left-over-right crossovers.

1

2

3

4

5

6

7

8

9

10

BASIC SLALOM

Learning how to slalom is fun, and it also helps you to refine your turning and edging techniques.

You can create your own slalom course by using colored plastic cups or specially made slalom cones, or by marking a course on the ground with chalk. Don't put the cones too far apart; about 4–6′ is a good distance. A slight incline will make it easier for you to perform slalom; when on level ground you must count on your skating speed as you approach the course to give you sufficient momentum to navigate it.

Before you skate into the course, stand still with your skates fairly close together and review the way in which you move onto your corresponding edges. Feel how the rotation of your hips pulls you onto your edges.

Skate towards the course. As you approach the first cone, keep your knees bent, and begin to roll you left foot slightly in front of you so that it leads you into the turn. When you come alongside the cone, lean your knees to the left while rotating your hips to the left. This will move you onto the outside edge of your left skate and the inside edge of your right skate. A small push with your inside edge will help you around the cone.

In order to move quickly into the next turn to the right, roll your right foot slightly forward, lean your knees to the right while rotating your hips to the right, and roll around the cone on the outside edge of your right skate and the inside edge of your left skate. Again, a push with your inside edge will help you to make the turn.

Slalom course

1

4

2

3

5

6

THE LUNGE

This is one of the real "weight-lifting" exercises for in-line skaters. It helps to strengthen your thigh and quadricep muscles while stretching your hip muscles and increasing their flexibility.

Hang on to a wall or railing. With your skates parallel, bend your knees and roll your right leg out behind you. You can actually roll onto the front wheel of your right skate.

As you roll your leg behind you, focus on how balanced you are on your left leg. Make sure your left knee is in line over your toes. Feel strong support right through the hips, as you position your chest in line over your left knee. Now repeat the exercise, this time rolling your left leg back.

Move away from the wall. Glide with your feet parallel, about 4–6″ apart. With your eyes and head up, and looking straight ahead, put your arms up in front of you as if hanging on to the wall or railing.

Wall lunge

Slowly bend your knees and roll your right leg behind you. Continue to lower yourself, concentrating on the point of balance over your left leg. Your chest should be over your left knee, and your knee over your toes.

As you lower yourself, you may actually roll onto the toe of your right skate. Only lower yourself as far as is comfortable.

Now repeat the exercise, this time rolling your left leg back.

SKATING BACKWARD INTO BACKWARD CROSSOVERS

Skating backward Before you begin, review the rocking horse exercise to remind yourself of the feeling of moving backward while pushing with your inside edges.

Backward walk Stand with your feet comfortably apart. Bend your knees, lower yourself into a sitting position, and turn your toes inward.

With your skates in the pigeon-toed position, begin to take small backward steps. Feel how you push off your inside edges. Keep your rear end down in the sitting position.

Backward scooter To move backwards around a circle in a clockwise direction, imagine a circle and rotate your head and upper body into the line of travel. Lower yourself almost to a sitting position, turn your right toe inward slightly, and push with the inside edge of your right skate. Your weight should be centered over your left, inside leg. Look over your left shoulder and continue pushing in order to move around the circle.

Now try moving backward around a circle in a counterclockwise direction. Look back over your right shoulder, center your weight over your right, inside leg, and push with the inside edge of your left skate.

The backward, "pigeon-toed" walk

Backward crossovers

You may not have to call upon your ability to perform backward crossovers during the course of a normal day of in-line skating, but this skill opens the door to very advanced skating maneuvers.

First, visualize the intended line of travel, clockwise around a circle. Lower yourself almost to a sitting position, and look back over your left shoulder as you begin to push with the inside edge of your right skate. Continue to scooter backwards. Your weight should be centered over your inside leg. Now begin to reach into the center of the circle of travel with your left skate each time you push with your right.

Once you're comfortable with this, reach into the center with your left skate one more time, pick up your right skate and cross it over the front of your left, making sure that your inside leg is strong and deeply bent. Bring your left leg back alongside your right to complete the backward crossover.

Now try it the other way: Moving counterclockwise, reach with your right leg into the center of the circle, and cross your left skate over your right.

1

2

5

3

4

Backward crossovers: Reach into the circle with that inside leg!

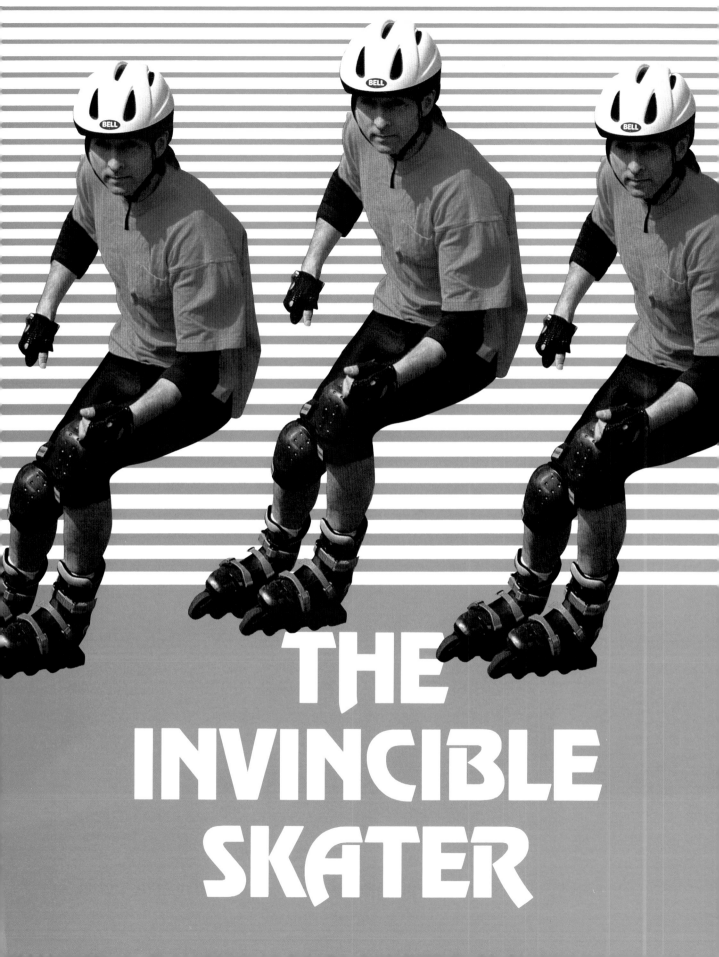

THE
INVINCIBLE
SKATER

IN-LINE POWERSKATING

On in-line skates, *powerskating* refers to the art of skating over any terrain without any interruption of balance or stride.

Here are a series of exercises and tips that are intended to help you with your balance, agility, flexibility, turning, and striding.

Deep knee bends
Use as balance warm-up and strengthener.

Deep knee bends

Knee lifts
Great for balancing and centering yourself over one leg at a time. Go slowly.

Knee lifts

Tight "airplane" turn
Works on your upper body and hip rotation. Focus on trusting your inside leg.

1

3

2

4

Corresponding-edge turns

Practise without the slalom cones! Works your hips and knees when you keep your feet as close together as possible.

3

1

2

4

Powerstriding

Strong efficient striding emphasizing strong inside edge push for maximum thrust. Keep working toward a longer glide.

Extend your rear leg all the way back. Pump your right arm forward when your right leg is doing the pushing. Pump your left arm forward when your left leg is doing the pushing. The more you bend your knees, the more powerful your stride will be.

Powerstriding: front view

Powerstriding: rear view

STREET SMARTS

Skating on the streets is really quite easy if you abide by a few simple rules.

If you have practised all of the exercises up to this point, you may find that you're ready to skate anywhere.

Warning! Before you begin skating in the street, read this chapter and practise all the techniques in a safe, uncrowded area away from cars and pedestrians.

When skating on the streets, you may encounter cracks in the sidewalk, cracks in the road, metal grates, rough pavement, manhole covers, curbs, inclines, cobblestones, gravel, dirt, brick side-

Foot in front onto grass or sand

walks, and a wide variety of bumps in all shapes and sizes. How will you overcome these obstacles?

The most important thing you can do is to keep one skate (preferably the one with the heel brake) in front whenever you're gliding. This will allow you to use your heel brake at a moment's notice, and it will also prepare you for any emergency that may arise. By keeping one foot in front of you, you create an extended wheelbase, which provides you with more stability should you suddenly have to roll into the grass, sand, dirt, or other nonskating surface.

If you have to glide into the grass (or some other nonskating surface) in order to avoid a pedestrian or other obstacle, slide one foot in front of the other, bend your knees, and roll into the grass.

Street smarts: foot in front!

To skate over a metal grate, . . .

simply get a foot out in front of you, . . .

bend your knees, . . .

and simply keep rolling!

Manhole covers

1

2

3

Roll over those obstacles! Foot in front!

Curbs When you come up against your first curb, stop and simply step either up or down the curb. With practice and confidence, you'll be able to take them in stride. Remember to keep your knees bent. *Never* straighten your legs when negotiating a curb.

Stairs Don't skate them! Walk them! Skating stairs is reserved for either the most skilled (or most daring) of stunt skaters.

Upstairs: Hold on to the railing and walk up the stairs with your toes in a "V" position. As you step onto each stair, roll your skate forward and jam your toe up against the next stair.

Walking downstairs

Downstairs Take the stairs backwards, holding on to the railing and making sure your toes are turned out. As you step down onto the next stair, roll your skate forward so that it jams into the step. Look where you're going!

Walking up stairs: Roll into that stair!

Uphills Skating uphill forces you to use proper skating technique; you have to be pushing with your inside edges in order to make it up the hill.

For easy uphill skating technique, make sure that you aren't sitting back on your heels. If you center your weight over the balls of your feet as you stroke up the hill, you'll notice an immediate increase in ease of skating and speed!

Uphill powerstriding

Don't sit back on your heels!

Downhills Don't take on the big hills until you're sure of your control and braking ability on smaller hills. When riding downhill, keep your braking foot in front of you, stay centered and balanced through your hips, and control your speed if necessary by making light contact with your heel brake. Keep your knees bent at all times and don't lean back. If you begin to feel out of control, *don't* wave your arms around and *never* straighten your legs. Instead, bring your hands to your knees, stay low, and try to use your brake.

You may soon find yourself being able to skate down hills on which you previously had to use your brake!

As your confidence increases when skating downhill, you may want to try gliding with either foot in front of you. If you're turning to the left, keep your left foot in front of you, and when turning to the right, keep your right foot in front of you.

TIPS

- Keep your eyes up and stay focused on the road ahead of you. Be prepared for the unexpected.
- Watch out for oil slicks on the roads. Avoid transit-bus lanes, as buses tend to leak engine oil and diesel fuel onto the road.
- Obey all traffic regulations. Don't dart in and out of traffic. It's hard enough for drivers to see you as it is.
- Be kind to pedestrians. Warn them about the side on which you intend to pass. *Always* yield to pedestrians!

STREET SKATING SAFETY TIPS

1. Always wear your protective equipment!
2. When skating, keep your knees bent, and your eyes up.
3. When gliding, be sure to roll one skate in front of the other. This will lengthen your wheel base, enabling you to make smooth transitions from one type of surface to another and to roll over small bumps and cracks without losing your balance.
4. When turning, make sure that both skates are making contact with the ground. Keep your eyes and upper body moving in the direction of your turn!
5. When stopping keep your braking foot well in front of you and maintain a near-sitting position. Never lean back!
6. When standing, never straighten your legs completely. Always stand with your knees slightly bent.
7. When approaching intersections, begin to slow down well before you get there. Look in every direction before proceeding!
8. Be aware of where you are in relation to other skaters, cyclists, and automobiles at all times. Avoid sudden lane changes.
9. Avoid wet or oily road surfaces. If you have no choice but to go through such an area, stay well centered over your skates and take small, light strokes.
10. If at any time you feel off-balance, bring your hands to your knees!
11. If you are feeling tired, don't skate.

THE HEALTHY SKATER

Because in-line skating uses so many muscles, begin each session by skating at a slow, easy pace for several minutes. You want to get the blood flowing to your muscles before you exert yourself.

Your skating warm-up should include:

- deep knee bends (while gliding)
- lunges (while gliding)
- swizzles
- scooters
- braking practice

Cool down & stretching As
with any form of exercise, it's important to do some stretching after skating. The best time to stretch is just after skating. Your muscles and blood are already warm, and your body will benefit the most under these conditions.

SKATE CARE

The manufacturer of your skates should provide the tools you need to maintain your brakes, wheels, and bearings. If these tools aren't provided, buy them at any skate shop.

HEEL BRAKE

Examine your heel brake periodically to be sure that there's sufficient rubber in the brake pad to bring you to a complete stop. Most manufacturers have a wear line indicating when the rubber brake should be replaced.

Look at the two skates with brakes in the following photograph. The brake on the left is in excellent condition; the brake on the right should be replaced.

The skate manufacturer should provide the tools you need to change your brake. You may also need a screwdriver.

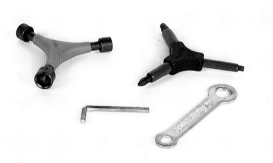

Various skate tools

Left skate: new brake pad; right skate: worn brake pad.

WHEELS

Rotating your wheels
If you skate indoors or on extremely smooth surfaces, your wheels will last much longer than if you skate on rough, uneven asphalt or pavement. Because you use the inside edges of your wheels the most, they'll begin to wear down first.

If you let this wear go unchecked, your wheels eventually look like this:

Worn-down inside edge

Worn wheels will lessen your speed and agility; they may even cause you to slip and fall. Compensation for worn wheels may also force your body out of good skating posture.

To prevent uneven wearing of your wheels, periodically rotate them and move them to different locations on the skate blade. A well-used, but frequently rotated wheel retains an overall, even roundness, and may last three to four times as long as a wheel which is not rotated.

Properly rotated wheel

An excellent rotation sequence is to move the front wheel to the back; then move each of the other wheels forward by one position.

As you change the position of each wheel, turn it so that what was previously the inside edge now becomes the outside edge.

New set of eight wheels

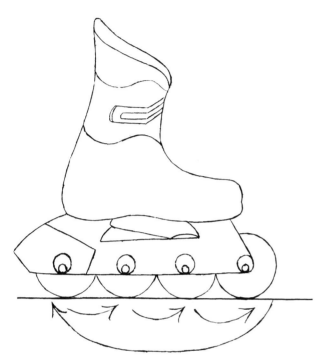

Wheel-rotation placement

Buying new wheels

When the time comes to buy new wheels, buy a set of eight.

It seems that new wheels appear on the market almost every day. Some of these wheels are made for specialized in-line skating forms, such as stunt, hockey, or speed skating; so choosing wheels can become quite a science.

When you bought your skates, the wheels supplied by the better-quality skate manufacturers were just fine! They were chosen as the best wheel design for the needs of the majority of in-line skaters. Use the size and hardness of the wheels that came with your skates for comparison when shopping for new wheels.

Wheel size

Recreational-wheel diameters range from 65mm to 82mm. The size of the wheel is marked on the wheel. The largest wheels are used by speed skaters. The smallest are best for stunt or dance maneuvers. Unless you plan to specialize in speed or stunt skating, you should buy wheels ranging from 72 to 76mm in diameter.

Wheel hardness

The other mark that you see stamped on a wheel refers to its durometer, or "hardness," rating. Durometer is indicated by the letter "A," with hardness ranging from 70A to 84A. A wheel durometer of 78A is suitable for almost any type of skating.

When buying new wheels, your decision as to what to buy is dependent on your skating style and demands. Once that's settled, go for the colors!

BEARINGS

You will see your bearings when you first rotate or change your wheels. The bearings that are supplied by the better manufacturers are of very high quality, and should last a long time before they are in need of any special care or eventual replacement.

Bearing quality is subject to an engineering standard known as the ABEC standard. The higher the ABEC number, the higher the quality of the bearing with regard to internal tolerances and evenness of rolling. Bearings rated at ABEC-1 or ABEC-3 are best for recreational skaters; make sure that your bearings are rated at least ABEC-1.

Try to avoid skating in areas with excess water, grease, sand, and oil. Skating in these conditions is dangerous; it will also shorten the life of your bearings. If you have to skate through a wet area, make sure that you continue skating on a dry surface for a while before you take off your skates. This will help to dry your bearings.

Insert bearing pusher tool into hole—push!

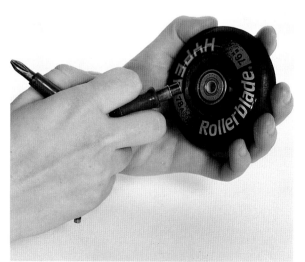

How to hold wheel and bearing tool

Removed bearing: You can see the axle spacer.

Typical serviceable bearings

Bearing care
Whenever you rotate your wheels, take a cloth and wipe off the grease and dirt that has accumulated on the bearings. In order to clean both sides of the bearings, you will need a special bearing tool in order to pop the bearings out of their hub sockets. This tool can be purchased from any in-line skate dealer.

Hold the wheel firmly in one hand. Put the round, blunt part of the special bearing tool into the hole in the bearing and give a good push. You will pop the bearing (along with the axle spacer) out of the other side of the wheel into the palm of your hand. Take a look at your bearing assembly to see how to put it back together. Now, pop the other bearing out of the hub as well.

After you have wiped off both sides of both bearings, push one of the bearings back into place in the hub. Place the axle spacer back into the middle of the hub and into this replaced bearing. Now, push the other bearing back into its place in the hub.

Bearing replacement or upgrade
If your bearings are making strange sounds or not spinning freely (or at all!), it is time to buy a new set.

You can replace them with factory bearings, rated ABEC-1 or higher, or with ABEC-rated serviceable bearings, with removable bearing-retainer shields that allow you to inspect, clean, and lubricate your bearings as needed.

SMART SKATING ACCESSORIES

Hip bag (and contents)
Carry the following items with you whenever you go skating:
- In-line tool (in case you need to make any emergency adjustments to your skates and wheels)
- Sunglasses
- Sunscreen
- Water or sports drink. You should drink water at least every 20 minutes while skating.
- Small first-aid kit (bandages and antibiotic ointment in case of a scrape)

Skate tote strap
An easy way to carry your skates to or from the skating area.

Power straps
If you need extra ankle support, you need power straps. Various sizes are available to fit either over the instep or around the ankle; each size is adjustable.

Crash pads

Crash pads are shorts that have hip and tailbone protective pads sewn into them. Designed for those who want extra protective padding, crash pads allow you to try more advanced maneuvers with minimal risk of injury during a fall.

Skate walkers

Many store owners (and transit systems) don't allow in-line skates to roll on their premises. Skate walkers stop your wheels from rolling; they allow you to walk as if in street shoes.

Skate tote

Crash pads

Hip bag

Power straps

Skate walkers

BEYOND THIS BOOK!

In-line stunt skating, in-line speed skating, in-line figure skating, in-line dance skating, in-line ramp and half-pipe skating . . .

There is always something to learn! If you are interested in expanding your in-line horizons, make friends with people who are experienced with other forms of in-line skating. Learn the basics of each discipline very thoroughly and, as you do so, remember: you are working muscles that don't usually get exercised unless you are on your skates. Go slowly and be kind to yourself! In-line skating demands that you combine systematic learning with a "go-with-the-flow" approach. As your natural balance improves, you will find that your innate ability to recapture and remember new movements improves as well.

The common in-line denominator, though, is *skating.* If you have worked your way through the exercises in this book, then congratulations are in order! You will rely on these in-line skating basics time and time again.

See you out there! Skate, skate, skate!

INDEX